TOGETHER WITH GOD

ENJOYING GOD ON THE JOURNEY OF LIFE

STEVE CHAPPELL

For information contact:
Coastline Baptist Church
557 Vista Bella
Oceanside, CA 92057
(760) 754-2302

Cover design by Matt Chappell
Layout by Jennifer Telles
Edited by L Words Editing Services

ISBN 978-0-9836713-1-2

Contents

INTRODUCTION

One day, when they were both still little girls, my daughters told me they wanted to help me wash our family's car. I've always been a stickler for a clean car, so of course I was a little hesitant. I looked over their heads at my wife, thinking, "Can you help me out here?" She answered back with a look that said, "Get over it. Go have some fun with your daughters."

Just three minutes into our car-washing adventure, they had dropped the washcloth in the dirt, knocked over the bucket, and hosed me off instead of the car. I often had to reach around them to fix a spot they'd "cleaned." But it was fun, and when we were done the girls were pretty happy to tell their mom, "Look what we did!" Did they? Well, yes: but they only succeeded by doing it "together with dad."

As I relate that memory to my heavenly Father I'm reminded that by His grace we are invited to live our lives with Him, for Him, and through His strength. Because He is God we know that He doesn't need us. But He loves us and He wants us to live our lives together with Him.

The apostle Paul enjoyed a life of intimate fellowship with God. His life took him many places, and in each step he was found in God's presence. On one occasion Paul wrote to the Christians living in Corinth, saying *"For we are labourers **together with God**: ye are God's husbandry, ye are God's building"* (1 Corinthians 3:9). It is my prayer that in these pages you'll gain some practical insights and encouragement to enjoy the greatest life there is: a life lived *"...together with God."*

CHAPTER ONE

WALKED WITH GOD

And Enoch lived sixty and five years, and begat Methuselah: And Enoch walked with God after he begat Methuselah three hundred years, and begat sons and daughters: And all the days of Enoch were three hundred sixty and five years: And Enoch walked with God: and he was not; for God took him.

--Genesis 5:21-24

The funeral service and reception had just ended and the thought of getting together with good friends for coffee seemed a good one. The group of men talked and laughed together, sharing memories of great times with their friend, and then one remarked, "So many people said so many nice things about his life. Kinda makes me wonder what people will say about me at *my* service."

Another answered, "I hope they say, 'He really loved his family.'"

The next man said, "I hope they mention my love for God."

The last man was the most pensive of the group, and slow to answer. His friends prodded, "So? What do you hope people will say about you when they see you lying in your coffin?"

He thought a minute more, then said, "I hope they say, 'Look! He's moving!'"

While a preoccupation with death can be unhealthy, a periodic assessment of how our lives are being lived can be of great value. There's a saying, "Only one life, how soon 'twill pass. Only what's done for Christ will last." Intentional living based on faith and the principles of God's Word blesses those we live with and those we leave behind and leads to a life well lived in the eyes of God. At the end of our race, we who know the Lord should desire above all to hear Him say, *"Well done, thou good and faithful servant"* (Matthew 25:21). But if we hope to hear "well done," we must do well.

Doing well begins with establishing an abiding relationship with Jesus Christ. This means accepting God's gracious offer of eternal salvation through faith in the work of Christ on the cross. But doing well continues as we go through life with Him each step of the way. We read in Psalm 37:23, *"The steps of a good man are ordered by the LORD: And he delighteth in his way."* And 1 Peter 2:21 says, *"For even hereunto were ye called: because Christ also suffered for us, leaving us an example, that ye should follow his steps."*

The Bible is filled with accounts of lives that serve as examples for us. Some teach us how not to live. Others' lives reveal a pattern that we would do well to emulate. One such life is that of a man named Enoch.

Although his life is mentioned a few times in the New Testament, his testimony is recorded for us in Genesis 5:

And Enoch lived sixty and five years, and begat Methuselah: And Enoch walked with God after he begat Methuselah three hundred years, and begat sons and daughters: And all the days of Enoch were three hundred sixty and five years: And Enoch walked with God: and he was not; for God took him.
--Genesis 5:21-24

Sometimes Christians use terms that lose meaning over time. "Walking with God" is one of those expressions. To "walk with God" is to understand the value of spending time with Him each day and throughout the day.

Each winter my wife, Lisa, and I take some time to get away from the rush of daily life and simply enjoy one another's company. We do a lot of the typical vacation activities, but one of our favorites is to begin each day with a long walk. We don't often take the time to walk together in our regular routine, so these getaway walks are special. They're not about the exercise, the locale, or even the destination. These walks are special because they're about our time together. As we walk, we talk about our family, our goals, and our future. We intentionally remove ourselves from all other distractions so we can communicate.

As the life of Enoch was reviewed in Scripture one statement stands above the rest: he is remembered as a man who *"walked with God"* (Genesis 5:22). Enoch enjoyed being with and communicating with God. And just like my walks with Lisa are about enjoying her company and sharing my heart with her, Enoch's walk was about sharing with God what was on his heart and, in turn, gleaning from the heart of God.

If we are to learn what it means to truly be "together with God," we should take note of some key elements of Enoch's walk.

Enoch's Walk Was Faithful

Clearly, there is much that we don't know about Enoch. We don't know what he did for a living. We don't know his wife's name. We don't know his hobbies. We know his father's name was Jared. We know he had a son named Methuselah, and we know that he lived an incredible 365 years. At that age, I'd say he earned his senior discount at Denny's!

Yet, twice in a span of three verses we read that Enoch *"walked with God."* The language suggests this was not a one-time or "on special occasions" occurrence. This man had a persistent and faithful walk. Although we don't know where the "walk" took place or what time Enoch and God met, we do know that it was a part of his routine in life.

That thought alone teaches us much. The prophet Amos rhetorically asked, *"Can two walk together, except they be agreed?"* (Amos 3:3) Did God walk with Enoch? Yes, He did. But, more significantly, "Enoch walked with God." That is to say that he decided to go wherever God was going and do whatever God would have him do. He made a conscious decision to invest in a relationship with God.

One evening not long ago I was relaxing at home on our sofa, my wife by my side. I was watching a Lakers game and texting the play-by-play to a friend, when Lisa said, "We need to spend some time together."

I was confused. Wasn't that what we were doing?

Lisa pointed out that my attention was on everything but her in that moment. And she was right. So I turned off the television, silenced my phone, and tuned in to her completely. It was the right response to show my wife that I value her and I value our relationship. I know that without an investment of time on a regular basis that we will naturally drift apart.

Enoch also knew this important principle. If we want to do life "together with God," we'll have to learn from Enoch that there is great value in making time in a busy world to simply be with Him.

Daniel was another man who enjoyed a close relationship with God. In fact, when he was thrown into a den of lions for his commitment to God, he was there with God – the best partner possible for such a predicament! Upon his release Daniel said, *"My God hath sent his angel, and hath shut the lions' mouths, that they have not hurt me: forasmuch as before him innocency was found in me; and also before thee, O king, have I done no hurt"* (Daniel 6:22). Daniel's relationship with God was not based on a one-time rescue from danger. He had a history of setting time aside every day to walk with God - through prayer: *"He kneeled upon his knees three times a day, and prayed, and gave thanks before his God, as he did aforetime"* (Daniel 6:10b).

I also think of David, the *"man after God's own heart"* (Acts 13:22). In his writings we find Psalm 55:17: *"Evening, and morning, and at noon, will I pray, and cry aloud: And he shall hear my voice."* Clearly, David thought enough of his time with God and the God of His time that he made it a priority in his life. He didn't just build time with God into his life; he built his life around his time with God.

Enoch was faithful in his walk. I think it is fair to wonder how that happened. Many who profess a desire to walk with God never actually get around to it. Others have seasons or moments of incredible closeness with God, but when life comes rushing in the closeness seems to get squeezed out.

There have been many times during my life when I really intended to walk with God. I love Him and want to live "with" Him. But time has a way of marching on and many times, just "intending" to do something is not enough. I've learned that what gets scheduled in my life gets done. I've never made it a habit to miss appointments, and when I set a standing appointment with God and stick to it I'm blessed in the process.

Make your time with God a priority in your life. Schedule it and stick to your appointments. As you do, you'll find your life developing a pattern of faithfulness that follows Enoch's example.

Enoch's Walk Was Focused

Genesis 5:22 begins, *"And Enoch walked with God after he begat Methuselah..."* Maybe it's the "dad" in me, but that statement touches my heart; when I read it, I just had to stop and think. In many ways, Enoch was much like us. He was no doubt a busy man, with the same demands on his time that we all have: work, bills, marriage, and being a dad. But his need for God did not diminish as his life got busier; in fact, it increased. So he continued to make his walk with God a priority.

I could not love my daughters more - they are wonderful. Psalm 127:3 reads, *"Lo, children are an heritage of the LORD: And the fruit of the womb is his reward."* My life has been enriched and blessed in so many ways by my children. The one thing they don't add to life is more time. In fact, they require a lot of it! I heard of one dad who felt bad about missing time with his kids due to work. To make himself feel better, he posed a question he thought he knew the answer to: "Kids, would you rather have quality time or quantity time?" To his surprise they answered, "Both!"

One mistake we may be tempted to make is to take from our time with God and give it to others. Of course, I'm not suggesting we should shortchange our families. But I am talking about a life that is focused on God. And I've discovered that when I spend my time with God, my time with others means so much more. You see, it is God Who teaches us how to make the most of each moment we have with our families. In Ephesians 6:4 we read, *"And, ye fathers, provoke not your children to wrath: but bring them up in the nurture and admonition of the Lord."* If it is a testimony to us to read that Enoch "walked with God" after his son was born, imagine what a great example Enoch's life was to his own children!

I use this matter of parenting to point out something bigger. The older we get, the busier we become. I haven't noticed life slowing down; in fact, our entire world clamors for our time. The world pressures us to be like them, and we can pressure ourselves to be liked *by* them. But that's a losing game. If you live for the approval of others you'll be a captive your whole life.

In Jude's short letter in the New Testament we find a mention of Enoch:

And Enoch also, the seventh from Adam, prophesied of these, saying, Behold, the Lord cometh with ten thousands of his saints, to execute judgment upon all, and to convince all that are ungodly among them of all their ungodly deeds which they have ungodly committed, and of all their hard speeches which ungodly sinners have spoken against him. (Jude 14-15)

Having delivered a few sermons in my time, I can assure you that Enoch didn't spend much time crafting those words so his audience would be happy with him. Rather, his focus was on God; he did and said what God wanted with all of his heart.

God never gives us more to do than time to do it, and when your focus is on Him He will help you order your life in such a way that the important areas are always covered. In addition to helping us know what to do, He also helps us know what doesn't need to be done. When you walk with God you'll always be where you need to be when you need to be there. He'll see to it!

Enoch's Life Was Fruitful

We've covered that Enoch walked with God; it may be the most obvious testimony from his life. But the writer of Hebrews adds to that testimony: *"By faith Enoch was translated that he should not see death; and was not found, because God had translated him: for before his translation he had this testimony, that he pleased God"* (Hebrews 11:5). Think of those final words, *"...he pleased God."* What a thought!

There are a lot of differing philosophies about how one can please God. Some say that we please Him by doing "good deeds." But the apostle Paul said, *"Therefore by the deeds of the law there shall no flesh be justified in his sight: for by the law is the knowledge of sin"* (Romans 3:20). Simply put, no number of good deeds you could possibly do would please God. Want to know what does please God? Hebrews 11:6 tells us: *"But without faith it is impossible to please him: for he that cometh to God must believe that he is, and that he is a rewarder of them that diligently seek him."*

Faith pleases God every time. It was Enoch's faith in God as the basis of his walk that led to the fruit of pleasing God. He was not walking with God to gain acceptance, but because he already had acceptance in Him. As Hebrews 11:6 says, Enoch came to God in faith, and God was pleased. If we are going to follow in the steps of Christ and thereby live life together with Him we must establish a relationship by faith and then walk with Him in faith.

Enoch's life had an interesting conclusion. Genesis 5:24 records, *"And Enoch walked with God: and he was not; for God took him."* It is clear that God welcomed Enoch into His Heavenly home, but how this all happened isn't clear. One minute, Enoch was here on earth, and the next, he wasn't. Some view this as an Old Testament picture of the rapture of the Church by Jesus Christ.

The best explanation I've read actually came from a young girl who learned the account of Enoch in Sunday school. As the story goes, when the girl's mother asked about the lesson, the girl replied, "We talked about Enoch."

"Oh, you did?" her mother asked. "What did you learn about him?"

"Well," the little girl began, "God would come by Enoch's house every morning and say, 'Enoch, would you like to go for a walk with me today?' and Enoch would say, 'Yes, I would.' I guess this went on and on for a really long time, and every day Enoch and God would walk a little farther than the day before. One day, they walked so far and it got so late that God said, 'Hey, Enoch, we walked a really long way today, and we're a lot closer to my house than yours. Why don't you just come home with me?' So, Enoch went home with God to His house."[1]

One day we will be able to ask God exactly how He welcomed Enoch home, but one thing is certain: this was quite a conclusion to quite a life. Enoch's life teaches us that believers have the promise of God's

---

1 answersfromthebook.org

presence for all eternity, but that doesn't start when we physically die. It can start now as we walk with God.

You can begin your walk with God today by first understanding your need for a personal Saviour. Romans 3:23 makes it very clear that we all have a huge problem called sin: *"For all have sinned and come short of the glory of God."* This simply means that none of us are perfect.

The problem with sin is that it has a high price tag. Romans 6:23a says, *"For the wages of sin is death…"* In other words, the price for sin is eternal death apart from God in a place called Hell. But because God loves us, He sent help! The rest of Romans 6:23 says, *"…but the gift of God is eternal life through Jesus Christ our Lord."* And in Romans 5:8 we read, *"But God commendeth His love toward us in that while we were yet sinners Christ died for us."*

Jesus Christ wants to be your Saviour. He came to earth as God in the flesh, lived a perfect life, and then voluntarily died on a cross because He loves you. In His death, He literally paid for all of your sins. The

Bible promises in Romans 10:13 that all those who *"call on his name shall be saved."* You have nothing to lose and everything to gain. Pray and ask Christ to be your Saviour and claim the eternal life found in Him.

A life spent together with God begins by establishing the greatest relationship a person can experience on this earth: a personal relationship with Jesus Christ. Only then can you know, as Enoch knew, the joy of pleasing God by walking with Him in faith.

CHAPTER TWO

THE WORD OF GOD

For the word of God is quick, and powerful, and sharper than any two-edged sword, piercing even to the dividing asunder of soul and spirit, and of the joints and marrow, and is a discerner of the thoughts and intents of the heart.

--Hebrews 4:12

Years ago, my boss asked me if I wanted to give up a day off to travel to look at a farm. You would have thought I'd have said, "Uh, no way." But I was excited. I wasn't excited to see a farm or take a drive – I've done that plenty of times. I was excited to spend time with a boss who had become a friend and mentor to me, someone who taught me something nearly every time we talked. I wasn't nearly as concerned with where I was going as the one with whom I'd make the journey.

When I traveled with my boss, I hung onto every word he said, expecting to gain a profound insight about business or life. Of course, this expectation wasn't always met. But when I travel with God I've found that He never fails. He always has a truth for me that can transform my life.

God's inspiration and instruction are found in His Word, the Bible. It is imperative that those who want to travel through life together with God take time to read the Bible. Jesus said, *"Search the scriptures; for in them ye think ye have eternal life: and they are they which testify of me"* (John 5:39). The word *search* literally means "to investigate[2]," which is what Paul intended

2 Smith's Bible Dictionary (Revised Edition). 1981. Zondervan.

when he told a young pastor named Timothy, *"Study to shew thyself approved unto God, a workman that needeth not to be ashamed, rightly dividing the word of truth"* (2 Timothy 2:15). Our relationship with Christ is so much more meaningful when we take time to listen through our reading of the Word of God.

I don't think anyone would be shocked to learn that as a Bible preacher and teacher, I'm a huge advocate of group Bible study. Spending time in God's Word does something for us that nothing else can do. At Coastline Baptist Church we gather on Sunday morning, Sunday evening, and during the week for the purpose of opening God's Word together so that we can learn and grow. But all too often, Bible study groups assemble to learn more *information* about the Bible. They learn about the human author, the primary audience, and the context of a text, but they miss the mark when it comes to communicating God's Word in such a way that it leads to changed lives.

D. L. Moody, a well-known preacher of the 1800s, once said, "The Bible was not given to increase our knowledge but to change our lives." It is good to get into the Bible, but it is better when we allow the Bible to get into us! When unleashed in our lives, God's Word has the capacity to perform spiritual surgery, transforming us over time to more closely resemble Jesus Christ in our words, deeds, and attitudes. Learning information may be a component of Bible study, but it's not the goal. Life transformation is our goal.

The Bible contains many commands and encouragements to participate in corporate study. The picture we find of the first century church was of a group who met often to study together: *"And daily in the temple, and in every house, they ceased not to teach and preach Jesus Christ"* (Acts 5:42). The writer of Hebrews said, *"Not forsaking the assembling of ourselves together, as the manner of some is; but exhorting one another: and so much the more, as ye see the day approaching"* (Hebrews 10:25).

But spiritual health and vitality do not come from simply taking what others feed you. Don't get me wrong; being fed is a big part of spiritual growth.

In fact, the role of a Bible teacher has been likened to that of a spiritual chef: *"Feed the flock of God which is among you, taking the oversight thereof, not by constraint, but willingly; not for filthy lucre, but of a ready mind"* (1 Peter 5:2). While the under-shepherd's job is to make sure the diet of the flock is well balanced and nutritious, at the end of the day the students must delve deeper for themselves.

I am thankful for the opportunity I had to go to Bible college. My school held weekly chapel services, during which I heard messages from some of the most well-known and respected preachers in the country. I also had incredibly gifted professors who left an impression on my life. But the best thing I learned in college was how to study for myself. My professors' goal was not to teach me everything I needed to know but to provide a foundation that would allow me to be a lifelong learner.

In a similar sense, my desire as a pastor is to teach the Bible in such a way that each member of our church family sees the value of studying for himself or herself beyond our group study. A life that is lived together with God hears from God through His Word. But first we must understand what we hold in our hands when we pick up a Bible.

The Nature Of God's Word

All scripture is given by inspiration of God, and is profitable for doctrine, for reproof, for correction, for instruction in righteousness.
--2 Timothy 3:16

The Bible is God's Word for mankind. A friend of mine used to say the letters of the word *Bible* stand for, "Basic Instructions Before Leaving Earth." This is certainly true, but the Bible also contains everything we need to know to live our lives here on earth.

The Bible is preserved. We learn from Hebrews 4:12 that *"The Word of God is quick."* *Quick* is a term used to speak of something that is alive. The apostle Peter explained that God's Word was given through inspiration: *"For the prophecy came not in old time by* *the will of man: but holy men of God spake as they were moved by the Holy Ghost"* (2 Peter 1:21). Writers of the Bible received the living and life-giving Word of God. And God's Word is still "quick"; it is alive today because God has promised to preserve it for us!

You can rest assured that the Bible does not just contain the Word of God; it is the Word of God. Jesus said, *"Heaven and earth shall pass away: but my words shall not pass away"* (Luke 21:33). The Psalmist said, *"The words of the LORD are pure words: As silver tried in a furnace of earth, purified seven times"* (Psalm 12:6). And Peter wrote, *"But the word of the Lord endureth for ever. And this is the word which by the gospel is preached unto you"* (1 Peter 1:25).

I heard a story of a mom who was sitting next to her daughter in church. Pointing to the mom's Bible, the girl leaned over and asked, "Did God really write that?"

The mom whispered back, "Yes."

In amazement the daughter replied, "Wow! He has really nice handwriting."

God did write His word for you! He gave us His word through inspiration and has preserved His truth as He promised.

The Bible is powerful. Hebrews 4:12 also tells us that God's Word is *"powerful."* The Bible has the power to change our lives. In His prayer to the Father, one sometimes called the High Priestly Prayer, Jesus said, *"Sanctify them through thy truth: thy word is truth"* (John 17:17). The word *sanctify* speaks of changing, and this change comes by way of the truth of God's Word. There is not a single issue in your life that God's Word doesn't address in power.

The Bible is perceptive. Finally, Hebrews 4:12 describes God's Word as *"sharper than any two-edged sword, piercing even to the dividing asunder of soul and spirit, and of the joints and marrow, and is a discerner of the thoughts and intents of the heart."* The Bible pierces and divides our soul and spirit. It distinguishes between the flesh and the spirit. It knows even the most secret matters of our hearts.

One day, following a Sunday service, a pastor stood at the back of his church to speak with folks as they left. One man remarked, "Powerful message today, Pastor. It was well structured and easily understood. I always see myself in your sermons."

"That's great," the pastor replied.

"Oh, that wasn't a compliment," said the man. "I want you to knock it off!"

The Bible is timeless and relevant to all of us. Like a "looking glass," or mirror, it shows us what is in our hearts and lives: *But we all, with open face beholding as in a glass the glory of the Lord, are changed into the same image from glory to glory, even as by the Spirit of the Lord"* (2 Corinthians 3:18).

This is the nature of God's Word. It came from God. He preserved it for us. And it has the power to change our lives.

The Need For God's Word

At least once a year, I drive from my home in California to visit my family in Colorado. When making my travel plans, I schedule my stops around my two major needs: fuel for my vehicle and food for me. Because I've made this trip dozens of times, I know exactly where to stop for both, which makes trip planning much easier. When it comes to our spiritual lives, the Bible is our one stop for the fuel and food that we need in life; not only that, it is our road map to chart our course when we're in unfamiliar territory.

I'm all for predetermined checkpoints and rest stops along the highway of life, but as we travel at a sustained pace we will find we need the Bible more than ever. As life gets busier and pressures mount, sometimes we complain of feeling "burnout." But I think many times our problem is not burnout, but "run out" – as in, run out of fuel and food. We must learn to regularly refuel and feast on the Bible to combat the pressures of life. Job, who knew a thing or two about pressure, said, *"Neither have I gone back from the commandment of his lips; I have esteemed the words of his mouth more than my necessary food"* (Job 23:12). Job learned that he could do without a lot of things in life, but he could not do without the support of God's "commandment."

Peter wrote, *"As newborn babes, desire the sincere milk of the word, that ye may grow thereby"* (1 Peter 2:2). Have you ever seen a hungry baby attack a bottle? You get the idea the baby is thinking, "If I don't get this bottle inside me *right now*, we're going to have a problem!" That is the same sense of urgency we are to have about God's Word. We simply need it in our lives.

Most Christians in this country have no shortage of Bibles in our homes; yet, too many of us fail to see our need for the Bible as we journey through life. The prophet Amos wrote, *"'Behold, the days come,' saith the Lord GOD, 'That I will send a famine in the land, Not a famine of bread, nor a thirst for water, But of hearing the words of the LORD'"* (Amos 8:11). Contrary to what we've been taught, the most important meal of the day is not breakfast; it's time spent in God's Word. We need the spiritual food we receive through studying the Bible at church and other places, but more importantly, we need the food received through our personal time with

God. His Word sustains and equips us to go through life together with Him.

The Nurturing Of God's Word

Have you ever been on the road, thinking you knew where you were going, only to get lost anyhow? I remember a time I was on my way to a speaking engagement. Already running late, I exited the freeway where I thought I was supposed to. After a few minutes of seeing nothing that looked familiar, I plugged my destination address into my GPS, only to have the device tell me that I wasn't even on a known road. The streets around me were newer than the software used by my GPS, which meant I was completely on my own. Not good!

We've all gotten off-track in life in some way or another; we all know what it means to find ourselves in a no-man's land that even our GPS can't figure out. If I were to poll people of faith and ask if they considered time in God's Word important for keeping us on the right road in life, I imagine nearly everyone would respond with an emphatic "Yes!" But if I then asked how many take time each day to hear from God through His Word, I'd get a different answer. Too many would say, "I know I'm supposed to. I know it's *good* to do. But I'm not currently doing it."

We sometimes say, "absence makes the heart grow fonder," but that is not always true. Sometimes absence makes the heart grow colder – and the more absent the Bible is from our daily lives, the more difficult it is to know how to get back to it. How do you start making steps toward getting (or getting back) into God's Word routinely? To steal a phrase from Nike, "Just do it!" Just making a decision to reopen the lines of communication will help you in more ways than you realize. In Psalm 119:9 we read, *"Wherewithal shall a young man cleanse his way? By taking heed thereto according to thy word."*

We don't grow to get in the Word; we get in the Word to grow. Let me challenge you to read your Bible every day. It will require a decision, and that decision will require discipline. But that discipline will lead to delight and a relationship that enriches your life.

John Kass, a columnist for the *Chicago Tribune*, recently wrote about a local waiter named Bouch who decided to write to the king of his homeland, Morocco.[3] King Mohammed VI is immensely popular because he interacts with his subjects in public, has freed political prisoners, and helps the poor and disabled. When he received Bouch's letter, King Mohammed VI wrote back.

Bouch was delighted. "Look at these letters from my king," he said. "If I meet him, I'll be so happy."

When Kass interviewed Chicago's Moroccan deputy counsel general, he found it is not unusual for King Mohammed VI to write personal letters to his subjects abroad. "It happens a lot," the official said. "He loves his subjects."

---

3 Lee Eclov, Lake Forest, Illinois; source: John Kass, "Waiter's Pen Pal Just a Cool Guy Who Runs a Country," Chicago Tribune (7-23-01)

The columnist mused, "How many guys hauling beer and burgers in a Chicago tavern have a correspondence going with a royal monarch?"

You ought to meet Jesus, the King of Kings, and read His precious letters to you.

Sometimes, it can be difficult to know where to begin. If you would like a free Bible reading plan, simply email *togetherwithgod@coastlinebaptist.org* and we'll send you what you need to get started.

CHAPTER THREE

TEACH US TO PRAY

I was going to a place I'd never been to do something I'd never done. The thought of making the trip alone seemed almost more than I could bear. So when my friend Arden offered to join me on the cross-country trek that would take me to my first year of college, I didn't have to think long. That first morning, pulling away from my home and all that was familiar was hard, but somehow knowing an exciting trip with a friend lay ahead made it easier. Along the way we encountered a tornado, flat tires, a couple opportunities to go fishing, and many other memories that will be with me for a lifetime.

Once you take a road trip with someone, you have a lifelong connection. Sharing a journey is sharing your life, or at least a part of it. But living life together with God is more than a cross-country trip or periodic encounters on Sunday mornings or special holidays. It can literally be a daily walk that adds more to our lives than we could imagine.

On a road trip, there is plenty of time for communication. Of course, communication is at least 50% listening. As we travel with God we get to listen to Him through His Word. God the Spirit communicates with our hearts as we read and dwell on the Scriptures: *"But the Comforter, which is the Holy Ghost, whom the Father will send in my name, he shall teach you all things, and bring all things to your remembrance, whatsoever I have said unto you"* (John 14:26).

But in communication, after you've listened you get to share your perspective or experience. And prayer is an integral part of our communication with God.

By definition prayer means "asking," but it includes much more than that. Prayer is literally sharing our heart with our God, Who is interested in hearing what we have to say. Few things say, "I love you" as much as giving your attention to someone. David knew this when he wrote in Psalm 5:3, *"My voice shalt thou hear in the morning, O LORD; In the morning will I direct my prayer unto thee, and will look up."* I don't find in those words a man who was bragging about his consistent prayer life; rather, I find a man overwhelmed that God loves us so much that He is there to hear us each time we come to Him in prayer.

Despite my relief all those years ago at having a friend along for my cross-country journey, if I never spoke a word to Arden as we traveled, it would be hard to say we made the trip together. In the same way, our prayer life is a major part of traveling through life with God. As our study continues, let's invest some time considering the value of a life of prayer.

The Lord's Prayer (Luke 11:1-4)

And it came to pass, that, as he was praying in a certain place, when he ceased, one of his disciples said unto him, "Lord, teach us to pray, as John also taught his disciples." And he said unto them, "When ye pray, say, Our Father which art in heaven, Hallowed be thy name. Thy kingdom come. Thy will be done, as in heaven, so in earth. Give us day by day our daily bread. And forgive us our sins; for we also forgive every one that is indebted to us. And lead us not into temptation; but deliver us from evil."

I wouldn't say I'm an introvert, but I am definitely quiet. At gatherings or in a crowd, I'm usually the guy in the back of the room listening to someone else's story. I've been told over the years that I'm a good listener, but while I'm quiet on the outside, there's usually a lot going on inside. In fact, my wife can tell you that it can be hard to get my attention if she wants me to listen, and the effort usually involves turning off a Los Angeles Lakers game!

Unlike me, God is always quick to listen. When we need Him, we always have His undivided attention. One of my favorite psalms is Psalm 40; in verse 1 David wrote, *"I waited patiently for the LORD; And he inclined unto me, and heard my cry."* The word *inclined* gives the word picture of someone leaning closely to hear every word. No one can communicate like our God, but He is also the greatest listener we'll ever meet.

Jesus Christ is God the Son. He became a man without ceasing to be God. Sure, He voluntarily laid aside some of the prerogatives of His deity, but He was all man and all God all at the same time. There were a lot of things Christ's followers would have found intriguing about Him. He had power over evil spirits. He could quiet storms with a word. He could heal the sick and captivate entire crowds with his teaching. But one thing about Christ that apparently stood above the rest was His prayer life. While living as a man He placed a premium on prayer. His disciples routinely found Him taking time, even prolonged periods of time, to talk with His Father.

When Christ's disciples asked Him to teach them to do what they saw Him do, they didn't ask for instruction on how to perform miracles; they asked, "Lord, teach us to pray." It was the closeness in His relationship with the Father that they sought. We sometimes say that there's power in prayer, but from Christ's example the disciples could see it is more accurately stated that there's power in the God to Whom we pray.

Many authors, myself included, have written books about the prayer that we often call The Lord's Prayer. It serves as a model. Although much could be said about every statement and word, I want to emphasize four truths that can help us as we seek to communicate together with God.

An Understood Command

I just love the way Jesus begins His instruction in prayer; He very gently says, *"When ye pray"* (Luke

11:2). The thought here is that not only do we need prayer in our lives, but there is also an expectation that we will pray – and often.

Christ's words could easily be made into the question, "When do you pray?" The first lesson I find here is that it would be helpful for us to establish a time to pray (remember: what gets scheduled gets done). Furthermore, Luke 11:1 tells us that when the disciples found Christ, "*… He was praying in a **certain place*.*" Jesus apparently had both a time and a place for prayer. In Matthew's recording of this occasion Jesus said, *"But thou, when thou prayest, enter into thy closet, and when thou hast shut thy door, pray to thy Father which is in secret; and thy Father which seeth in secret shall reward thee openly"* (Matthew 6:6). The point is not that you need a special closet in which to pray. But it is helpful to set aside a season and space for your communication with God.

There is not a person alive that I love more than my wife. She is my best friend, bar none. But as much as I love her, I could easily get so busy doing other things that I miss out on the more important matter of talking with her. And even the best of relationships crumble without communication. This is why we schedule those daily walks during our annual getaways. For the other days of the year when we're not on vacation, we set aside specific times in the day and we schedule regular date nights to just talk and enjoy one another's company.

Similarly, it is helpful to establish a time and place so you can talk with God regularly. The implication from Christ's words is that we absolutely need this in our lives.

A Unique Connection

When we come to God in prayer as people of faith we get to begin by saying, "...*Our Father*" (Luke 11:2). What a privilege! The Bible says, "*We love him, because he first loved us*" (1 John 4:19). God is the prime mover in establishing our relationship with Him. We are "born again" by faith into His family, which makes Him our Father. But unlike any of our earthly fathers or like those of us who have the privilege of being dads, our Father is perfect and full of love. There is never a time we cannot come to Him and there is never a topic we cannot talk to Him about.

I used to laugh at people who said their dog was like a family member, but after being a dog owner, I understand. Our dog, China, grew up with my children, and we all loved her dearly. When I would come home in the evenings, China was almost always thrilled to see me. Sometimes, however, she was nowhere to be found. That usually meant she had done something bad earlier in the day. Because she was a dog, she couldn't understand that hiding from me was not the best strategy. Our paths always crossed eventually, so whatever she'd done would be dealt with before long.

I've noticed that Christians can be the same way in our prayer lives. Sometimes when we are guilty or convicted about something, we feel as though we can't enter into God's presence through prayer, so we withdraw. But God has never thrown any of His children out of His throne room; He knows that is the very place we most need to be. Paul tells us, *"Let us therefore come boldly unto the throne of grace, that we may obtain mercy, and find grace to help in time of need"* (Hebrews 4:16).

Grace is God's unmerited favor, and the very throne that God sits on is called "the throne of grace." Our loving, merciful, and gracious God will correct and redirect us at times, but because of our unique connection by faith we have a relationship that will never end.

An Unconditional Commitment

In Psalm 124 David recounts some trials in his life, but he bookends his story with praise for the Lord's intervention, acknowledging, *"If it had not been the Lord Who was on our side"* (Psalm 124:1, 2). When we understand that we serve a God Who has an unconditional commitment to us we, too, will be encouraged to respond to Him. When you enter into His throne room in prayer and see that His throne is a throne of grace you'll come to understand that His way is always best.

A sincere heart in prayer will say, *"Thy kingdom come. Thy will be done, as in heaven, so in earth."* As I shared in my book, *When You Pray*, "Prayer is not about getting our will accomplished through the power of heaven. Prayer is about getting God's will accomplished in our lives on earth." A committed heart in prayer seeks to honor God. A committed heart longs for God's work to be accomplished.

Recently, one of my daughters approached me for advice about a problem she was dealing with. As we talked she said something that grabbed my attention: "Dad, I've already decided I'm going to do whatever you think is best." She went on to explain that she understood that she did not understand. I knew what she meant because I've been there many times myself! But as she said it I thought, "That's the heart I'm to have towards my Heavenly Father." My daughter reminded me that we are to come to God predetermined to do what He thinks is best.

This attitude was exemplified so perfectly in the life of Christ. Shortly before His crucifixion we find Jesus in a garden, praying: *"And he went a little further, and fell on his face, and prayed, saying, O my Father, if it be possible, let this cup pass from me: nevertheless not as I will, but as thou wilt"* (Matthew 26:39). Christ's prayer was premised upon a decision to do His Father's will.

Unifying Change

"And forgive us our sins; for we also forgive every one that is indebted to us." (Luke 11:4)

Prayer is a vertical thing. By that, I mean prayer is between you and God. But the results of living life "Together With God" in prayer have horizontal ramifications. We've heard it said that prayer changes things, but the greatest change that comes when we pray is the change inside us! When you accept forgiveness from God it liberates you to forgive others. After all, how can I talk to God about forgiveness if I am harboring a grudge towards others?

In Matthew 18, the Lord told a story about a king who decided to collect from a man who owed him a large sum of money. When the man could not pay, the king ordered that he, his wife, and children all be sold into slavery to satisfy the debt. The man pled for mercy, and the king graciously granted it. But read what happened after the man who'd just been forgiven left the king's presence:

> *But the same servant went out, and found one of his fellowservants, which owed him an hundred pence: and he laid hands on him, and took him by the throat, saying, Pay me that thou owest. And his fellowservant fell down at his feet, and besought him, saying, Have patience with me, and I will pay thee all. And he would not: but went and cast him into prison, till he should pay the debt. So when his fellowservants saw what was done, they were very sorry, and came and told unto their lord all that was done. Then his lord, after that he had called him, said unto him, O thou wicked servant, I forgave thee all*

that debt, because thou desiredst me: Shouldest not thou also have had compassion on thy fellowservant, even as I had pity on thee? And his lord was wroth, and delivered him to the tormentors, till he should pay all that was due unto him. So likewise shall my heavenly Father do also unto you, if ye from your hearts forgive not every one his brother their trespasses. (Matthew 18:28-35)

What is clearly illustrated here is that, of all people, people of faith should be forgiving. Paul said, *"And be ye kind one to another, tenderhearted, forgiving one another, even as God for Christ's sake hath forgiven you"* (Ephesians 4:32). God has freely and fully forgiven our sins; how can we then withhold our forgiveness from others?

When we pray we see God for Who He is, ourselves for who we are in Him, and others through the lens of God's grace and forgiveness. We are reminded by our acceptance into His throne room that we are there by

His grace, and we can extend that grace to others in our lives. Prayer makes the difference.

When my daughter asked my advice for her problem, I've already mentioned that I was struck by her determination to follow whatever course I deemed best. But what was also interesting was that she seemed to already know what advice I would give her. Maybe she knew it because we've talked enough over the years that she's got her old dad figured out. But I've found that the same thing happens when I go to God in prayer. The more time I spend talking with Him, the more I understand His heart and will for my life. Of course, understanding God's heart does not diminish my need to live "Together With God" by consistent prayer. Rather, it adds meaning and depth as I do.

If you would be interested in learning more about prayer, there are many resources available. One such resource is the book I referenced earlier entitled, *When You Pray*. To get this resource, please email us at ***info@coastlinebaptist.org***.

CHAPTER FOUR

GOD SHALL SUPPLY

How much of your time is spent dealing with money? I'd say a lot! Most people work a minimum of forty hours a week to earn it. Then we spend time (at least I hope we do) budgeting and planning how it should be spent. We take time to shop, time to balance our checkbook, and take time to think down the road about retirement or major purchases. Even watching the news can make us wonder how current events may affect our bottom line. Any way you slice it, money is a major part of our lives.

Money is also an intensely personal subject. There seems to be an invisible line from our wallets that connects to our hearts. The Bible explains it this way: *"For where your treasure is, there will your heart be also"* (Matthew 6:21). I've noticed that when the topic of money is broached, sometimes walls go up. But the reality is that God has a lot to say about our financial lives. He owns it all, and He wants to help us be effective managers of His many blessings.

It has always seemed strange to me that some would desire to include God in their lives through Bible study and prayer but exclude Him when it comes to finances. God's Word reveals that our money works best when we manage it with Him. The Bible is filled with principles of financial management that work for every person in every conceivable situation. One verse in particular stands out as a great place to start learning how to conduct our financial lives "together with God":

> *"But my God shall supply all your need according to his riches in glory by Christ Jesus."*
> --Philippians 4:19

The global economy, including our own, has undergone some incredible challenges in recent years. Many people who previously counted on the performance of their portfolios for security in retirement saw values diminish greatly. Others have found that the job market is much tougher and that available jobs don't provide as they once did. These challenges can lead people to believe that if they just had more money they would have more security.

We tend to think that people who seem to have plenty of money have it made. But often people who have more tend to worry more; they have more to insure and more to lose. The Bible helps us to understand that, for the person of faith, security comes not from money, but from a greater source. Our security comes from God.

It is ironic that our money bears our national motto, "In God We Trust" when we are all too often more likely to have put our trust in money instead. Looking to money for security leads to a loss of confidence and peace. God wants to help us in those areas. Philippians

4:19 begins, *"But my God **shall** supply **all** your need..."*
The word *shall* means something much stronger than
"will"; it means, "there's no doubt about it[4]." And the
verse says He'll supply *"all"* our needs. That is a great
promise. But it's a promise with a premise. To see all of
our needs met we must handle our finances according
to His plan. How can we know God's financial plan for
our lives?

The Principle Of Confession

To understand how God wants us to use the resources
He has blessed us with, we must first invite Him into
this realm of our lives by confessing that we need His
help. The Bible is filled with invitations to come to
God for help. Jesus said, *"Ask, and it shall be given you;
seek, and ye shall find; knock, and it shall be opened
unto you"* (Matthew 7:7). James, the half-brother of
Jesus, said it this way: *"Ye have not, because ye ask not"*
(James 4:2b).

---

4 Smith's Bible Dictionary (Revised Edition). 1981. Zondervan.

For years I've heard the saying, "Before you pay, pray," yet I had to be reminded of it some time ago when I called my oldest brother for financial advice. After we talked he asked, "Have you prayed about it?" At first, his question irritated me. I thought, "I'm coming to you because you have more experience and knowledge then me!" But my brother did the best thing he could have done. He pointed me to someone with more experience and knowledge.

How much trouble could we save ourselves if we asked, "Have I prayed about it?" before making financial decisions? If our God has promised to supply all our needs, why would we try to shoulder the burden of trying to figure out how to supply our own needs? That's a load He did not design us to carry.

When we ask God for help in our finances we can be assured that not only is He much more experienced in money matters, but that He is always ready for our call. I recently spoke with a man who makes his living as a financial planner. He gave me his card and told me, "Call me anytime if you have questions." I appreciated the offer, because there is value in the service he provides. But his words were not entirely accurate. I've left more messages than I can count! But when I follow the principle of confession and invite God into my financial life I don't have to leave a message and hope He calls me back; He is right with me each step of the way.

The Principle of Contentment

When we paint our financial picture we want to be as comfortable as possible. That's understandable. But when God evaluates our pictures He is more concerned with our *contentment* than our *comfort*. God knows that the world's system lures us to desire more and more without ever getting ahead. When was the last time you bought a new car and a newer, better model was *not* released just a few months later? Technology is even worse; if you buy a new computer or cell phone tomorrow morning, there will be a newer model on the shelf practically before you even get home. We just can't keep up!

The only way to win this rat race is to opt out altogether. We do this through contentment. The apostle Paul said in Philippians 4:11, *"Not that I speak in respect of want: for I have learned, in whatsoever state I am, therewith to be content."* Paul knew that when he had God, he had enough. He did not come naturally by this knowledge of contentment. He said, *"I have **learned**."* This is an area of life in which we all can grow.

I used to view contentment as a lackadaisical, almost fatalistic approach to life. But contentment does not mean that we work less or stop striving for the dreams and goals God has given us; those actions are not rooted in faith. Contentment means we learn that happiness is not connected to a bank balance. It means we realize that, as my grandmother often says, "The best things in life aren't *things*."

When we lack contentment we are looking for that next promotion or purchase to bring us joy. But it never works. When we acquire the thing we wanted so badly, we are often immediately looking for the next big thing. Friends, things just don't do it for us! Like Paul, we must learn contentment. Hebrews 13:5 reads, *"Let your conversation be without covetousness; and be content with such things as ye have: for he hath said, I will never leave thee, nor forsake thee."* When we learn contentment we'll know that when we are journeying through life with God, we have all we'll ever need.

The Principle Of Chronology

This principle speaks of the "first things first" approach to our finances. The first thing isn't food, shelter, or even taxes. The first thing is giving. Solomon wrote, *"Honour the LORD with thy substance, And with the firstfruits of all thine increase"* (Proverbs 3:9). I'm not sure why God established our financial management as a test of our faith, but He did. And He wants to be first in all that we do.

Our giving to God affects every other area of our lives. Regarding giving an offering, the apostle Paul said in 2 Corinthians 9:6, *"But this I say, He which soweth sparingly shall reap also sparingly; and he which* soweth bountifully shall reap also bountifully." This is known as the law of the harvest: we reap *what* we sow, we reap *after* we sow, and we reap *more* than we sow.

Coming from a long line of farmers, I understand this principle. If you plant a seed you reap a plant that is full of seeds. The way to have your needs met in this sense is to give a seed and let the results follow. Jesus said, *"Give, and it shall be given unto you; good measure, pressed down, and shaken together, and running over, shall men give into your bosom. For with the same measure that ye mete withal it shall be measured to you again"* (Luke 6:38). The law of the harvest doesn't make much sense in our economy because it requires faith. But in God's economy, faith is to lead the way.

As we think of the local church, the church you attend, we know that God has established giving as His method of financing His work on earth. He asks us to give the first ten percent of our increase, a practice we call *tithing*. Tithing was seen in the Old Testament before the Law and during the Law, and in the New Testament. The apostle Paul wrote, *"Upon the first day of the week let every one of you lay by him in store, as God hath prospered him, that there be no gatherings when I come"* (1 Corinthians 16:2). The first day of the week is Sunday, and God's expectation is that each of us worships Him through giving *"as God hath prospered."* As we often say, "It is not equal giving, but equal sacrifice."

God does not ask us to give because He is short on money. Tithing is not His way of getting what's yours. Everything we have is His to begin with – and when we are disobedient in the matter of giving, we are trying to keep for ourselves what belongs to Him. Malachi 3:8 reads, *"Will a man rob God? Yet ye have robbed me. But ye say, Wherein have we robbed thee? In tithes and offerings."* And 1 Timothy 6:7 emphasizes the point that we were given everything we have: *"For we brought nothing into this world, and it is certain we can carry nothing out."*

The reason God wants our giving is that He knows real giving comes from the heart. It is the heart that God is seeking. The Bible says, *"Every man according as he purposeth in his heart, so let him give; not grudgingly, or of necessity: for God loveth a cheerful giver"* (2 Corinthians 9:7). God loves *"cheerful"* givers that give to Him from their hearts. If we are not cheerful about giving, we would do better to hold onto "our" money, because pressure and guilt never lead to true giving. Love is to lead the way in our giving.

Our regular giving to God through tithing of our income is a weekly reminder of our God Who is good and has provided all that we have because of His great love and care for us. The principle of chronology helps us to keep first things first.

The Principle Of Character

God honors that which honors Him; dishonesty and rash financial decisions do not honor the Lord or the resources that He has placed in our hands. If we are dishonest with our work ethic, taxes, or our agreed-upon payments, we remove ourselves from God's promise to *"supply all your need."*

Dishonesty robs us of joy. Even when we think we are getting ahead, we always fall behind when we gain something dishonestly. In Proverbs 16:8 we read, *"Better is a little with righteousness than great revenues without right."* To that Jesus adds, *"For what is a man profited, if he shall gain the whole world, and lose his own soul? or what shall a man give in exchange for his soul?"* (Matthew 16:26)

The principle of character also covers unwise spending that leads to consumer debt. King Solomon taught his sons, *"The rich ruleth over the poor, And the borrower is servant to the lender"* (Proverbs 22:7). There is incredible pressure in our culture to keep up with those around us. Too often, people get swept away by the credit card mentality that places such a burden on us that we go deeper and deeper into debt.

God has promised to provide for our needs, and if a purchase is truly a *need,* we would do much better to save up and pay for it once than charge it and pay interest over and over. Maybe you're in a situation now in which keeping up your credit payments is getting tough. Cut up the charge cards, develop a plan, and begin paying them off. (If you'd like help getting your finances on track, please contact us at ***togetherwithgod@ coastlinebaptist.org*** and we'll gladly send you some helpful materials.)

God's promise for our provision does not cover poor financial decisions on our part along the way. Treat your finances with great care. Remember that God is the owner of our resources; we are just the managers. Manage well!

The Principle Of Confidence

"But seek ye first the kingdom of God, and his righteousness; and all these things shall be added unto you."
--Matthew 6:33

The verse with which we began our study was a promise to those who gave to equip the work of God.

If they followed in obedience, they could mark it down that God would care for them.

When I was growing up, I went to my Dad whenever I had a need. I never worried about my next meal, if I'd have clothes after my next growth spurt, or if I'd have a home in which to live. That was his worry. Now I have children of my own and they aren't worrying much about whether their needs are met, either. Providing for them is my job. In fact, if my girls walked around the house stressed out all the time, I would be insulted.

Our Heavenly Father has promised to meet our needs. What are we communicating to God when we worry rather than trusting in His promise? When we live as if meeting our needs were all up to us we are little different than atheists in many ways.

By "Seek ye first the kingdom of God," God is saying, "Follow my plan for your life and I'll take care of the rest." We read in 1 Timothy 6:17, *Charge them that are rich in this world, that they be not highminded, nor trust in uncertain riches, but in the living God, who giveth us richly all things to enjoy.*" Who is "rich in this world?" Comparatively speaking, we all are. Not only do we have a God in Whom we can trust, but we are commanded to do so.

And if you can trust Him with the material needs in your lives it may be good to be reminded that you can trust Him with your eternity. The apostle Paul was a man who endured much, but there was also a sense of confidence in his life. He said, *"For the which cause I also suffer these things: nevertheless I am not ashamed: for I know whom I have believed, and am persuaded that he is able to keep that which I have committed unto him against that day"* (2 Timothy 1:12). Paul knew that no matter what challenges he faced in life, God was more than able to care for him. He will care for you, too!

CHAPTER FIVE

HE AROSE AND FOLLOWED HIM

And as Jesus passed forth from thence, he saw a man, named Matthew, sitting at the receipt of custom: and he saith unto him, Follow me. And he arose, and followed him. And it came to pass, as Jesus sat at meat in the house, behold, many publicans and sinners came and sat down with him and his disciples. And when the Pharisees saw it, they said unto his disciples, Why eateth your Master with publicans and sinners? But when Jesus heard that, he said unto them, They that be whole need not a physician, but they that are sick. But go ye and learn what that meaneth, I will have mercy, and not sacrifice: for I am not come to call the righteous, but sinners to repentance.

--Matthew 9:9-13

Although initiative and hard work are a part of any accomplished life, no one can claim to be self-made. Innumerable people and experiences have shaped each of our lives. As I look back, I see a host of others who have invested in my life. Without their influence I would be a different person.

Of course, I've been blessed with a loving family and some true friends. But I also see others, like my Junior Varsity basketball coach, Ray Clifton, who encouraged me, and my Junior High English teacher, Mrs. Preston, who gave me an appreciation of the English language. I also think of Mrs. Dalton, my college writing teacher. She had such a great way of teaching us to craft our thoughts and ideas. I specifically recall her calling me up on the final day of class to tell me that my score of 96% on my final paper was the highest she had ever given and that she was proud of me. I'm almost embarrassed to share with you how much that meant to me.

We all have moments in time when we can recall how someone made an impact on our lives by reaching out in one way or another. It has been said that you can impress from a distance, but to make an impact you must be close. The greatest impact we can make on others is to share the hope that we find in Christ.

If you are a believer, you have God to thank. He convicts and draws us by His Spirit. But no doubt, there were others who contributed through their words and deeds. For me, although I heard the gospel many times growing up, it was a sermon from a visiting pastor that provoked me to trust Christ. Although he may not know it during his lifetime, that pastor did the single greatest thing for me that any person can do for another.

Our good works do not spiritually save us, but we have been saved to do good works. The Bible says, *"For we are his workmanship, created in Christ Jesus unto good works, which God hath before ordained that we should walk in them"* (Ephesians 2:10). And, there is no greater work than obediently following the Lord's command to share the gospel message with others. It is our privilege to serve as a witness of the salvation that we entered into by grace and through faith.

We have a great example of what it means to be a witness of salvation in Christ's apostles. If you were to set their words aside, these men's very lives gave great witness to the message of Christ. The apostles left established lives of their own to live and ultimately die for the truth they found in Him. Matthew was one of these men.

When we first meet Matthew, in chapter 9 of the gospel he penned, he is working as a tax collector. His job supported the Roman Empire, which was not at all popular in his Jewish hometown of Capernaum. In fact, because tax collectors made their fortunes by overcharging citizens who had no real recourse for complaint, this occupation was nearly synonymous with being a thief.

One day as Jesus left a home in Capernaum, he passed by Matthew while he sat at *"the receipt of custom."* This started as just another workday for Matthew, but it would prove to be a day that changed his life. You see, on this day, he would trade in his career of collecting taxes for Rome to seek souls for the Savior. He responded to the call of Christ by arranging a dinner party for his companions and contemporaries so they too could meet Christ. He began that day to live the life of a witness for Christ, and we can learn much from his example.

A Personal Conversion To Christ

Matthew would have known of Christ and His message before the day that Christ called, *"Follow me."* In addition to being Matthew's hometown, Capernaum was the headquarters for Christ's earthly ministry.

I would imagine that there was some shock when Christ singled him out. Keep in mind that

Christ's other apostles were businessmen in that same community and given the choice, they most assuredly would have passed Matthew by rather than approach him. But Jesus loves people more than anything and He can save anyone. Was Matthew a sinner? Sure he was, but the Bible teaches us *"where sin abounded grace did much more abound."* (Romans 5:20)

Matthew knew what it was to meet the love of Christ in a personal way. The Bible shares a principle that those who've been saved by a merciful and gracious Savior tend to share that news with others. In fact, this is one of the great evidences of salvation!

Maybe you remember the account of the Maniac of Gadara, the demon-possessed man who was saved by Christ. After his conversion he wanted the whole world to know: *"And he departed, and began to publish in Decapolis how great things Jesus had done for him: and all men did marvel"* (Mark 5:20). Decapolis was a region consisting of ten cities, yet this man's witness for Christ reached them in such a profound way that *"all men did marvel."*

If you know that you have the forgiveness of sins, the assurance of a home in heaven, and the joy of living this life with God, then let others know! I think of King David, who painted such a vivid picture with his words:

I waited patiently for the LORD; and he inclined unto me, and heard my cry. He brought me up also out of an horrible pit, out of the miry clay, and set my feet upon a rock, and established my goings. And he hath put a new song in my mouth, even praise unto our God: many shall see it, and fear, and shall trust in the LORD.
(Psalm 40:1-3)

If we truly understood, like David did, the *"pit"* from which we've been lifted, we'd want to write about it, sing about it, and share that news with others. Matthew's witness began with his personal conversion to faith in Jesus Christ. He knew the isolation and sin of the life he'd been called from, and this spurred his eagerness to invite everyone he knew to come and meet Jesus for themselves.

A Passionate Commitment To Christ

At the invitation of Christ, Matthew *"arose and followed Him."* The miracle of this moment led to a life that was forever changed. He left a lucrative career, life as he'd known it, and ventured into the unknown just to follow Jesus. In Luke's accounting of this occasion we read, *"And he left all, rose up, and followed him"* (Luke 5:28). That's quite a thought. Matthew left everything to passionately follow Christ for the rest of his life. I wonder: what have you left in order to more closely follow Christ?

I think the main reason we often resist Christ's urging to serve Him, especially as His witnesses, is that we think we'll lose out in some way. But in Matthew's life, we find obedience lead to the unfolding of a life of adventure and purpose. Some years later Jesus asked this question to his followers, Matthew included: *"And he said unto them, When I sent you without purse, and scrip, and shoes, lacked ye any thing? And they said, Nothing"* (Luke 22:35). These men left everything; yet, they lacked for nothing.

You can pursue a lot of things in life and never gain a thing. But if you live for Jesus you'll find a life before you that defies logic and declares a witness. Matthew made the best move of his life that day!

A Perceived Compassion From Christ

With great brevity and humility, Matthew's narration moves ahead quickly. First he follows Christ and in the next word, they are together at a dinner party. Matthew's home, I'm sure, was larger than most. His guest list would naturally have included a list of "who's who" of Capernaum, including other tax collectors. Luke's gospel adds some detail to the picture: *"And Levi [Matthew] made him a great feast in his own house: and there was a great company of publicans and of others that sat down with them"* (Luke 5:29). Lest there be any misunderstanding about the nature of this crowd, consider Mark's accounting: *"And it came to pass, that, as Jesus sat at meat in his house, many publicans and sinners sat also together with Jesus and his disciples: for there were many, and they followed him"* (Mark 2:15).

Why would Matthew have invited Jesus to come to a house full of sinners? I think the answer is found in the final words of Mark 2:15 (*"...and they followed him"*). Matthew invited a group of sinners to his home because he was one of them. He was a tax collector who was as crooked as the others until he met Jesus and his life was changed in a moment of amazing grace and faith. He wanted his friends, those he had the most in common with, to have an opportunity to meet Jesus. As Christ had compassion for Matthew, Matthew had compassion on others.

This is the calling of all who are Christians. We are to love others as we have been loved. It really gets no clearer than the most familiar verse in the Bible, John 3:16: *"For God so loved the world, that he gave his only begotten Son, that whosoever believeth in him should not perish, but have everlasting life."* To people of faith Jesus said, *"A new commandment I give unto you, That ye love one another; as I have loved you, that ye also love one another"* (John 13:34). Jesus loves you, and He wants His love to touch others through you. One of the greatest evidences that Matthew understood Jesus' love for him, was the fact that he loved others like Jesus did.

A few years ago, I was blessed with the privilege of visiting the mission work of Rick and Becky Martin in Ilo Ilo, Philippines. One Saturday, I traveled with Mrs. Martin, some fellow guests, and a group from their church to a "squatters village." I must confess that between the heat, the smell, and the extreme poverty in that village, I wanted to keep my distance from those I met. But as they led Bible clubs with singing and teaching, I watched Mrs. Martin and her team offer hugs and one-on-one time to those they met.

As I later reflected on that experience, I was overwhelmed with the knowledge that these people loved as Jesus does and "together with God" they were changing lives one person at a time. Can we not do the same in our corner of the world?

A Profound Comprehension Of Christ

As beautiful as the picture of bringing others to Christ is, it's incomplete without mentioning the naysayers and critics who also made an appearance at Matthew's dinner. Interestingly, the critics were the religious people of the day. Matthew writes, *"And when the Pharisees saw it, they said unto his disciples, Why eateth your Master with publicans and sinners?"* (Matthew 9:11) The religious leaders weren't interested in love; they were interested in their own rules. But from his own experience Matthew knew that Jesus meets people where they are and changes their lives.

Nowhere in the Bible did Jesus command people to meet a standard before His love and grace would kick in. His love is a non-negotiable constant. As long as a person has breath, they have opportunity to accept His love. In response to the critical Pharisees Jesus said, *"They that be whole need not a physician, but they that are sick. But go ye and learn what that meaneth, I will have mercy, and not sacrifice: for I am not come to call the righteous, but sinners to repentance"* (Matthew 9:12-13).

Matthew just happened to believe that no one was beyond the love of God. If he could just get them to a place where they could meet Jesus, they would learn of His love and be changed just as he had been. And he was right.

At the end of Matthew's account of Christ's earthly ministry, he records Jesus giving His Great Commission to the church:

And Jesus came and spake unto them, saying, All power is given unto me in heaven and in earth. Go ye therefore, and teach all nations, baptizing them in the name of the Father, and of the Son, and of the Holy Ghost: Teaching them to observe all things whatsoever I have commanded you: and, lo, I am with you alway, even unto the end of the world. Amen.
(Matthew 28:18-20)

Our world is filled with people who need the love of Jesus, not our condemnation or criticism. Will you, like Matthew, reach out to them in love and introduce them to the Savior?

I worked for a time at a business in the Los Angeles area. Like most business environments, it was pretty diverse. I shared an office with a man who had an obvious drug problem and was also juggling two different immoral relationships. One night I was leaving the office to attend a men's function at my church. I invited my office mate without really expecting him to come, but to my surprise, he showed up.

As the evening unfolded, I decided I was going to share the gospel with him. But he surprised me again by getting my attention during the invitation that night and telling me he wanted to accept Christ. As we talked later that evening he shared, "I was shocked that you'd invite someone like me to come to your church." While the sermon convinced him of his need for Jesus, my invitation is what touched his heart.

What do you think would happen if we who have been touched by the love of Christ shared it with others? I believe God would use us to bring the lost to Him, and He can save anyone! But the first step is to learn from the example of Matthew, who, at the first call of Jesus, *"arose and followed Him."*

CHAPTER SIX

PEACE AMONG YOURSELVES

And we beseech you, brethren, to know them which labour among you, and are over you in the Lord, and admonish you; And to esteem them very highly in love for their work's sake. And be at peace among yourselves. Now we exhort you, brethren, warn them that are unruly, comfort the feebleminded, support the weak, be patient toward all men.

--1 Thessalonians 5:12-14

Family dynamics can change, sometimes dramatically, several times throughout our lifetimes. Having been born into a family and established one of my own, and now working with families on a regular basis through my local church, I've noticed that some family events require extra wisdom. One such event is the birth of another child.

Of course, welcoming the first child requires a lot of adjustments, but often the second child presents the first with a whole new world. Things like sharing time, toys, and attention are all new. It is not uncommon for the first child to resent this intruder. Parents are wise to spend time preparing for these changes and working diligently to distribute their love and time.

As we've studied this matter of going through life "Together With God" we have to understand that *together* refers to more than just God and you. There is a family dynamic at work as well. You see, all of us who have been "born again" (John 3:7) through faith into God's family are the children of God. That makes us all related. And journeying "together with God" means that we also have each other as traveling companions.

A large part of sharing our life with God is learning to share our lives with the body of Christ. So it is imperative that we learn the value of fulfilling our role as siblings in the faith. Being human, we have the capacity to be as petty as toddlers fighting over a toy. But being Christian, we also have the capacity, as we yield to God, to love one another as we have been loved. Just as we can find security through expressing and receiving love in our physical families, we can find great strength in life through giving and receiving love in our family of faith. This is one great purpose of our time together. The author of Hebrews wrote, *"And let us consider one another to provoke unto love and to good works: Not forsaking the assembling of ourselves together, as the manner of some is; but exhorting one another: and so much the more, as ye see the day approaching"* (Hebrews 10:24-25).

You learn a lot of lessons in the course of starting a church, and one lesson I learned early on was announcing an event that is special and meaningful to me doesn't necessarily make it so for everyone else. I discovered this as I prepared to introduce our first-ever guest speaker. Pastor Dwight Tomlinson, a long-time friend, made the trip from his much larger church to our living room for our mid-week service. We were a new church, so our numbers were understandably small, but on that night it seemed that most of our church was unable to attend.

As Pastor Tomlinson began to speak that night to what I considered an embarrassingly small congregation, I sat feeling smaller than I'd ever felt in my life. I should have been listening carefully while my friend shared the message God laid on his heart, but I had a hard time hearing over the voice in my head telling me that I'd been foolish for inviting a guest speaker for such a small crowd. I was sure that as soon as the message ended he would run to his car and regret having ever come.

To my surprise, not only did Pastor Tomlinson not hurry to get away afterwards, he stayed and talked with everyone until the last person left. When everyone else had gone he asked me to accompany him to his car, a Buick Roadmaster that may be the largest car ever produced. His back seat and trunk were filled with groceries for my family. There's no way he could've known it, but those groceries could not have come at a better time: my family had no food and no money to buy any. As we made trip after trip from his car to our kitchen, I felt a wave of relief and thankfulness that our family would now be able to eat for some time.

Once the groceries were unloaded we sat down and my friend began to share his impressions of our new church. He told me, "This is great! You're off to a good start and there are some wonderful people here." He went on and on, and each word was a treasure for me, a young pastor who had been rapidly becoming discouraged. By the time our conversation ended it was as though someone had put the wind back in my sails and I was ready to move ahead once more. He was a total blessing to me. I can't confirm that I would have quit without his words, but I can tell you that he made a great difference in my life that night.

I want you to know that I can think of many similar occasions when a brother or sister in Christ entered my life to help me. Sometimes help came by way of a correction; sometimes through encouragement. There were even times when the help wasn't in something that was said but a willingness to just listen when I needed to talk. I thank God for the joy of going through life not only with Him, but also with my spiritual family.

The apostle Paul's letters to the church in Thessalonica were directed to people who had already endured much in the way of persecution for the faith. In his first letter he said, *"For ye, brethren, became followers of the churches of God which in Judaea are in Christ Jesus: for ye also have suffered like things of your own countrymen, even as they have of the Jews"* (1 Thessalonians 2:14). But as is so often the case, the trials they suffered did not stop their influence for Christ. Paul's reflection on their ministry led him to write, *"Remembering without ceasing your work of faith, and labour of love, and patience of hope in our*

Lord Jesus Christ, in the sight of God and our Father" (1 Thessalonians 1:3).

Paul wrote 1 Thessalonians 5:12-14, our passage for this chapter, to encourage the church in their relationships within the family of faith. He was teaching them that just as unity and fulfilling our roles are necessary in biological families, they are an integral part of living "Together With God."

The Role Of A Pastoral Leader

My family bought a new car not too long ago, after hours of research and visiting multiple dealerships. When we finally made our decision and I sat down with the salesperson to begin the paperwork, he asked, "So Steve, what do you do for a living?"

I said, "I'm a pastor."

He laughed. "I can see why you haven't brought that up yet. I don't like to tell people I'm a car salesman, either."

Perhaps I should have brought it up sooner, but that conversation really underscores the view of pastors in America today. Our text begins, *"And we beseech you, brethren, to know them which labour among you, and are over you in the Lord, and admonish you; And to esteem them very highly in love for their work's sake."* The word *beseech* speaks of an earnest plea, and the plea was that the church would understand the role of a pastoral leader. The pastoral leader is to provide structure and *admonish* (to teach and/or warn) those he leads.

It saddens and disappoints me when those who fulfill the role of pastor are self-serving and abuse their office. This is clearly not the biblical criterion for godly leadership. To pastors Paul said in 2 Timothy 2:24, *"And the servant of the Lord must not strive; but be gentle unto all men, apt to teach, patient."* Biblical leaders are to lead as Jesus led, and He is our selfless Savior. But despite the stories we have all heard of pastors who abuse their leadership roles, I can tell you with a degree of knowledge on the topic that the overwhelming majority of pastors are men who love God, love His Word, and love those they serve.

Godly pastors fulfill their role by walking with God through Bible reading and prayer (Acts 6:4), preaching the *"whole counsel of God"* (Acts 20:27), and providing "oversight" of the local church. The word *pastor* means "shepherd," and Peter wrote that pastors are to *"Feed the flock of God which is among you, taking the oversight thereof, not by constraint, but willingly; not for filthy lucre, but of a ready mind"* (1 Peter 5:2). There have been some who have reacted to a negative church experience by discounting the role of pastoral leadership, but the Bible is clear that pastors who follow the Word are a blessing and deserving of appropriate respect. The writer of Hebrews adds, *"Obey them that have the rule over you, and submit yourselves: for they watch for your souls, as they that must give account, that they may do it with joy, and not with grief: for that is unprofitable for you"* (Hebrews 13:17).

There is great value in the life of a believer who has the influence of godly pastoral leadership. In the local church setting, this includes not only the senior pastor but, also, those who *"labor in the Word"* (I Timothy 5:17) to teach the truth and warn of error.

The Rule Of A Peaceful Living

One of the greatest gifts a church can give their pastor is to heed Paul's words, *"And be at peace among yourselves."* (1 Thessalonians 5:13b) What was he saying? He was telling those who are "together with God" to be "together" with one another as well.

The *"peace"* Paul spoke of is something that we let rule in our lives. Colossians 3:15 instructs, *"And let the peace of God rule in your hearts, to the which also ye are called in one body; and be ye thankful."* Just as some choose to be ruled by their anger, people of faith are to be ruled by peace. If this were easy, it would not have been emphasized so often in Scripture. This peace comes from the presence of the Spirit, and we must die to self to experience it.

I've heard it said that "the Gospel light attracts strange bugs," and sometimes that can definitely be true. People can try your patience and get under your skin. It always saddens my heart when I hear of a church that is enduring conflict or infighting, especially when these disagreements are rooted in petty preferences. It should not be this way. I'm not implying that believers must or will agree on every matter, but if we are to be ruled by the peace of God in our hearts we have to acknowledge another "rule": *"Nevertheless, whereto we have already attained, let us walk by the same rule, let us mind the same thing"* (Philippians 3:16). The *rule* mentioned there is the Bible, our sole authority in all matters of faith and practice. Our agreement is not found in personality or preference but in the principles of the Word of God.

I've told people many times over the years that I will gladly change anything being done at Coastline that contradicts something in the Bible. My goal as a pastor is not to get my way, but to do His will. Peace in the family of faith is something that we welcome as we yield to God's will.

The Responsibility Of A Participating Life

It is clear by Paul's words that he is addressing the family of faith. In verse 14 he says, *"We exhort you, brethren."* Brothers share a father, and Christians share God as our Father. But the tone of Paul's remarks changes somewhat as he continues: *"...warn them that are unruly, comfort the feebleminded, support the weak, be patient toward all men."* This tone is more like that of a commanding officer addressing his troops. We learn from this that we are in an intense spiritual warfare. To the Ephesians Paul said, *"For we wrestle not against flesh and blood, but against principalities, against powers, against the rulers of the darkness of this world, against spiritual wickedness in high places"* (Ephesians 6:12). And in Philippians we also learn that we are called to participate in this warfare.

One of the primary analogies the Bible uses to refer to believers and humanity in general is the analogy of sheep. Of Jesus we read, *"But when he saw the multitudes, he was moved with compassion on them, because they fainted, and were scattered abroad, as sheep having no shepherd"* (Matthew 9:36). And one of the primary analogies of the devil is that of a lion; Peter warned, *"Be sober, be vigilant; because your adversary the devil, as a roaring lion, walketh about, seeking whom he may devour"* (1 Peter 5:8).

Sheep have no defensive skills or weapons. They stand no chance in a fight with a lion. Sheep do best in the environment of the fold. If we are to be effective in spiritual warfare, we are not to live the life of faith as the Lone Ranger out in the pasturelands by ourselves – that is a sure way to see defeat. Rather, we are to participate with one another. In this context we are encouraged by and able to encourage fellow believers.

The Requisite Of A Profitable Love

How are we to encourage each other as we share our lives together with God? The last words in our text give clear instructions. Paul says first, *"Warn them that are unruly,"* and here, *unruly* is a military reference speaking of a soldier who falls out of rank or is walking out of order. A loving believer will reach out to those who've wandered from the protection of the Shepherd. If you are one who has wandered, recognize that while it may not be enjoyable, correction is needed in all of our lives at times.

Paul continues, *"comfort the feebleminded."* This expression literally speaks of encouraging people who are "weak souled," or those who become easily overwhelmed at various events in life. Sometimes we are that person! But all of us have opportunities to comfort those around us in their times of distress.

The next instruction is to *"support the weak."* In this context, *weak* refers to a soldier who is under attack or on the front lines. The word *support* has an interesting definition. It means "to hold oneself opposite," and it gives the same picture as what happens when you prop a bike on its kickstand. We are to "prop up" other believers when they are under attack. How thankful I am for those who've provided comfort and support during times in my life when I needed it!

Paul's final direction is that believers *"...be patient toward all men."* Yes, it says *"all"*! Without patience we have no persistence. This is a work in progress and it requires our commitment.

Not long ago a friend emailed me a link to a video with the subject line reading, "You have got to see this!" The video was an amateur recording of a confrontation between a group of African lions and water buffalo. The lions had singled out a stray baby buffalo as their prey, and they began to attack it. They circled the calf and pounced, and it looked as though things would end badly. But to my amazement, the herd of buffalo rushed together to the aid of the calf. Within seconds, they had pushed back the predators and restored the fallen to their midst.

What a great picture of what families, and particularly the family of faith, can do for one another!

Living life "Together With God" brings the blessings of family – brothers and sisters in the faith – to our lives. There is safety in numbers, and for believers, that number is one. We are safe as we draw close to God together, working alongside and supporting each other in unity and peace.

CONCLUSION

According to Bible historians, the Apostle Paul may have traveled as many as 18,000 miles throughout his missionary journeys[5]. During his years of travel, Paul did not lack for exciting and often dangerous adventures; he wrote in 2 Corinthians 11:25, *"Thrice was I beaten with rods, once was I stoned, thrice I suffered shipwreck, a night and a day I have been in the deep."*

I'm sure when Paul began his ministry journeys he never could have imagined the places God would

---

5 The Many Journeys of St. Paul – Apostle to the Gentiles. (www.agapebiblestudy.com)

lead him. But despite the dangers he encountered along those 18,000 miles, the strength he drew from his close walk with God not only sustained him but led him to impact countless lives.

Life is a journey, and as we travel it together with God, we too will be able to go to places we never could have imagined. But as we step out in faith to follow God, learn how to communicate with Him through prayer and study of His Word, and trust Him to supply all our needs, we will find the true joy of the journey is not in the great stops along the way; it's the One we get to travel with.

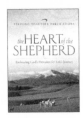

The Heart of the Shepherd
Embracing God's Provision for Life's Journey

This book explores the twenty-third Psalm to show how God's Word gives us a beautiful and encouraging portrait of our relationship with Him. He calls us His sheep and Himself our Shepherd. Not one step of your life's journey has escaped His loving guidance and protective care.

A Compassionate Christmas
Experience the Greatest Story Ever Told

Over two thousand years ago, the greatest event of all time took place when God wrapped Himself in human flesh and came to dwell with men. In these pages, you will find a biblical look into the plan of a loving Father to change the destiny of mankind through the ultimate gift: Jesus Christ.

When You Pray
Communicating on a Higher Level

The Lord's Prayer is perhaps the most familiar prayer in all of the Bible, yet it is likely the least understood. *When You Pray* is a thorough but practical look into the model prayer of Jesus Christ. Whether you have a fervent prayer life or are just starting your walk with Christ, this book will give you biblical principles for communicating on a higher level.

To order, please contact us at: info@coastlinebaptist.org